CRaZY NaTuRe™

Animals with Pockets

Marie Racanelli

PowerKiDS press™

New York

To Jessica

Published in 2010 by The Rosen Publishing Group, Inc.
29 East 21st Street, New York, NY 10010

First Edition

Editor: Joanne Randolph
Book Design: Greg Tucker
Photo Researcher: Jessica Gerweck

Photo Credits: Cover John William Banagan/Getty Images; p. 5 © www.iStockphoto.com/Karon Troup; pp. 7, 15, 17, 19 Shutterstock.com; p. 9 © John Cancalosi/age fotostock; p. 11 © Biophoto/Heuclin Daniel/Peter Arnold Inc.; p. 12–13 © J & C Sohns/age fotostock; p. 21 Gary Randall/Getty Images.

Library of Congress Cataloging-in-Publication Data

Racanelli, Marie.
   Animals with pockets / Marie Racanelli. — 1st ed.
       p. cm. — (Crazy nature)
   Includes index.
   ISBN 978-1-4358-9385-6 (library binding) — ISBN 978-1-4358-9862-2 (pbk.) — ISBN 978-1-4358-9863-9 (6-pack)
   1. Marsupials—Juvenile literature. 2. Pockets—Juvenile literature. I. Title.
   QL737.M3.R33 2010
   599.2—dc22

                                                    2009036517

Manufactured in the United States of America

CPSIA Compliance Information: Batch #WW10PK: For Further Information contact Rosen Publishing, New York, New York at 1-800-237-9932

Contents

What Is a Marsupial?

Our world is filled with countless animals. They come in many sizes, from tiny beings that we cannot see without special tools to huge elephants and whales. They come in many colors and shapes, too. They take care of their young in different ways and eat different things as well.

Some of these animals belong to a group called **mammals**. Cats, dogs, lions, and elephants are mammals. People are mammals, too! Did you know that some of the world's most unusual animals belong to a group of mammals called **marsupials**? Let's find out more about these animals with pockets!

Marsupials, such as this opossum, are animals that have pocketlike pouches. Their babies nurse and grow in these pockets.

Lots and Lots of Marsupials!

There are more than 250 **species** of marsupials. They include kangaroos, wombats, koalas, and others. They can be as small as a mouse or as large as a 6-foot (2 m) tall man. Most marsupials live in and around Australia. Some can be found in other places, such as South America or North America, too.

Depending on the species, marsupials can live in trees or on land. Some like to dig, and others like to climb. One marsupial even lives in water part of the time. Some hop, some run, some glide, and a few sleep a lot and hardly move at all!

Like other mammals, marsupials are warm-blooded, have hair, and feed milk to their babies. This is a marsupial called a quokka.

Pocket or No Pocket?

Most marsupials have a fully **developed** pouch, where their babies live and grow after they are born. Marsupial babies are still underdeveloped when they are born. They need special care in order to live. Most of them make their way into their mothers' pouches for this care, but not all of them do.

Some marsupials do not have a pouch. They are still marsupials because their babies are born at such an early point in their development. The numbat and the antechinus are both marsupials that do not have pockets. Once one of these babies is born, it finds and fixes itself to its mother and drinks milk from her body.

Numbats are pocketless marsupials that eat termites. They generally give birth to four babies, which hold tight to their mother's belly for six months.

Trip to the Pocket

When baby marsupials are born, they are pink and about the size of a large jellybean. They cannot see or hear, and they are hairless. They are not ready to be on their own yet, not even close! The only parts of newborn marsupials that are well developed are their front legs and their sharp claws. The claws help them hang on to their mothers as they climb to the pocket.

Once they get to the pouch, they fix themselves to their mother and begin to drink milk. The milk feeds them and helps them grow. Baby marsupials need to stay in the pouch to keep warm and stay safe from their enemies.

This tiny cuscus, which is a kind of Australian possum, will stay in its mother's pouch for six to seven months.

Crazy Marsupial Facts!

1 One of the most well-known marsupials is the kangaroo. A group of kangaroos is called a mob.

2 A baby kangaroo is called a joey. Actually, all baby marsupials are called joeys!

3 A few marsupials have become **extinct** in the last 100 years. The marsupial wolf and the thylacine, also called the Tasmanian tiger, are now extinct.

4 Most marsupials are **nocturnal**, which means they sleep during the day and hunt and eat at night.

5 Kangaroos and koalas get water from the food they eat. Because of this, they do not need to drink water often, if at all.

6 Most mammals have 20 to 40 teeth. Most marsupials have 30 to 50 teeth.

7 A kangaroo's pouch, which is near the kangaroo's stomach, opens at the top. Mother koalas, opossums, and wombats have pockets that open near their tails.

8 A wombat's poop is shaped like a cube! When it dries, it becomes very hard and it can be used as a building block.

9 Tasmanian devils leave no part of the animals they eat behind. They eat the meat, bones, and hair!

Tree Marsupials

Many marsupials, such as the sugar glider and the opossum, live in trees. Sugar gliders like to drink the sap of acacia trees and some kinds of eucalyptus trees. They also eat nectar, pollen, and some bugs. They glide between trees using the thin skin that stretches between their hands and feet.

Koalas eat only the leaves of eucalyptus trees. Koalas have strong claws, two thumbs on each hand, and rough skin on their feet. All these things help them be very good tree climbers. However, eucalyptus leaves do not give koalas much energy, so they move slowly and sleep for about 18 hours each day.

Strong arms and shoulders help a koala climb 150 feet (46 m) to the top of a tree and help it jump from treetop to treetop.

On Land and in the Water

Some marsupials, such as bandicoots and quokkas, like the ground better than the trees. Marsupials called Tasmanian devils live on land, too. They are hunters, but they will also eat dead animals. They have strong jaws and sharp teeth. Sometimes a group of them will snarl and scream at each other as they eat.

There is only one **aquatic** marsupial, though other marsupials can swim. These water marsupials, which live in places from southern Mexico to northern Argentina, are called yapoks. When a yapok is underwater, it keeps its babies safe by closing its pouch using a powerful **muscle**.

This is a Tasmanian devil. The screams of a Tasmanian devil can be heard from miles (km) away.

Meet the Wombat

Another land marsupial is the wombat. There are two kinds of wombat, the common wombat and the hairy-nosed wombat. These **vegetarian** marsupials like to burrow. Even the hardest dirt is no match for their strong, clawed front feet. Wombat burrows can be 100 feet (30 m) long. Wombats come out at night to graze on grasses and other plants.

Wombat joeys stay in the pouch for up to 10 months before they begin coming out for short amounts of time. They will return to the pouch for up to another 3 months before starting to eat grasses. Joeys stay with their mothers for about two years in all.

Wombats have pockets with openings that face toward their tails. This way, the dirt cannot get into their pockets when they are digging.

A Closer Look: The Kangaroo

Kangaroos are probably one of the world's most well-known pouched animals. They are known for their big feet and thick tails, which help them as they jump from place to place. They are plant eaters, and they have special teeth that help them bite off and chew the grass and leaves that they eat. There are 63 kinds of kangaroos, including the grey kangaroo, the red kangaroo, the wallaby, and the quokka.

The largest kangaroo is the red kangaroo. It can grow to be about 200 pounds (90 kg) and between 5 and 6 feet (1.5–2 m) tall! The red kangaroo is so powerful that it can cover about 30 feet (9 m) with each jump.

A kangaroo joey generally stays inside its mother's pouch for six to eight months.

Marsupials Close to Home

The only marsupial in North America is the Virginia opossum. Do not let its name fool you. This opossum lives throughout much of the United States. Opossums live in trees and come down at night to find food. They will eat nearly anything, including bugs, fruit, and seeds.

No matter where they live, marsupials are interesting animals. Unlike the opossum, though, many marsupials are in danger of becoming **endangered** or extinct because of hunting, predators, and **habitat** destruction. It is important for us to learn as much as we can about marsupials and to respect and keep these strange, wonderful animals safe.

Glossary

aquatic (uh-KWAH-tik) Living or growing in water.

developed (dih-VEH-lupt) Grown.

endangered (in-DAYN-jerd) In danger of no longer living or existing.

extinct (ik-STINGKT) No longer lives or exists.

habitat (HA-beh-tat) The place where an animal or a plant naturally lives.

mammals (MA-mulz) Warm-blooded animals that have backbones and hair, breathe air, and feed milk to their young.

marsupials (mahr-SOO-pee-ulz) Animals that generally carry their young in pouches.

muscle (MUH-sul) Part of the body that makes the body move.

nocturnal (nok-TUR-nul) Active during the night.

species (SPEE-sheez) One kind of living thing. All people are one species.

vegetarian (veh-juh-TER-ee-un) An animal that eats only plants.

Index

Web Sites

Due to the changing nature of Internet links, PowerKids Press has developed an online list of Web sites related to the subject of this book. This site is updated regularly. Please use this link to access the list:

www.powerkidslinks.com/cnature/pocket/

24